DADDY'S O[...]

Copyright © 2019 by Kimberly Roberts
ISBN 978-0-578-61475-5

All rights reserved. No part of this publication may be reproduced, distributed, or transmitted in any form or by any means, including photocopying, recording, or other electronic or mechanical methods, without the prior written permission of the publisher, except in the case of brief quotations embodied in critical reviews and certain other noncommercial uses permitted by copyright law.

For permission requests, write to the publisher,
addressed "Attention: Permissions Coordinator," at the email address below.
kimrobertsbooks@gmail.com
Ordering Information: Quantity sales.
Special discounts are available on quantity purchases by corporations, associations, and others.

Orders by U.S. trade bookstores and wholesalers.
Please contact Kimberly Roberts:
kimrobertsbooks@gmail.com
Printed in the United States of America

Mr. Ken greeted his student's parents for the first time during Back to School Night.

He stood before the class and said, "I'm pleased to meet you and excited to have your child in my class this school year."

Toya appeared to be sad as she and her mom left the school.

Her mom asked, "Is everything okay?" Toya looked at her mom with tears in her eyes and said, "I wish Daddy could've come with us tonight."

When Toya arrived home, she immediately ran to her Grammie saying, "I'm sad Daddy couldn't come to Back to School Night with me. All of my friends Dads were there."

Toya's Grammie comforted her by saying, "Sweetie remember Daddy is on Time Out! I'm sure he would've loved to go to Back to School Night with you and Mommy. He will be able to spend time with you at school again soon."

The next day at school Marquis broke one of the classroom rules and Mr. Ken placed him on Time Out. Marquis had to sit in the corner during class time.

During recess Marquis told Toya, "Mr. Ken is mean! I wasn't the only person breaking the rules in class today. I don't know why he put me on Time Out."

Toya explained, "My Daddy's on Time Out. My Mommy and I visit him a lot. I'm afraid when we go visit him because it's loud and it takes a long time to get inside. Once we're inside I feel happy because I get to spend time with my Daddy."

"When it's time to leave I become sad and sometimes I cry. I hug my Daddy and he tells me he loves me and reminds me that Time Out is making him better."

When the students returned to class after recess, Mr. Ken reminds them to follow the rules or they'll end up on Time Out.

Toya turned to Marquis and said, "I told you Marquis! Mr. Ken has classroom rules to help us stay focused.

Remember Time Out gives us time to think about what we've done."

The End

This book is a gift to my Grands

Dedicated in memory of my beloved Dad,
Ken Roberts, Sr.

About The Author

Kim Roberts is a mother, grandmother, and friend. She was born and raised in Richmond, California.

As a young girl she enjoyed reading and writing. Her debut children's book "Daddy's on Time Out" was inspired by a real-life situation that drew her family closer.

Her grandchildren are her inspiration who give her a reason to write children's books. Kim is passionate about encouraging her grandchildren and other youth to become avid readers at an early age.

Made in the USA
Las Vegas, NV
30 September 2022